BASS PLAY-ALONG

AUDIO ACCESS INCLUDED

EASY SONGS

Tracking, mixing, and mastering
by Jake Johnson & Bill Maynard at Paradyme Productions
Bass by Tom McGirr
Guitars by Doug Boduch
Keyboards by Warren Wiegratz
Drums by Scott Schroedl

To access audio visit:
www.halleonard.com/mylibrary

3069-5233-9765-6256

ISBN 978-1-4234-9122-4

HAL•LEONARD
CORPORATION
7777 W. BLUEMOUND RD. P.O. BOX 13819 MILWAUKEE, WI 53213

Visit Hal Leonard Online at
www.halleonard.com

CONTENTS

Bass Notation Legend

Bass music can be notated two different ways: on a *musical staff*, and in *tablature*.

THE MUSICAL STAFF shows pitches and rhythms and is divided by bar lines into measures. Pitches are named after the first seven letters of the alphabet.

TABLATURE graphically represents the bass fingerboard. Each horizontal line represents a string, and each number represents a fret.

3rd string, open | 2nd string, 2nd fret | 1st & 2nd strings open, played together

HAMMER-ON: Strike the first (lower) note with one finger, then sound the higher note (on the same string) with another finger by fretting it without picking.

PULL-OFF: Place both fingers on the notes to be sounded. Strike the first note and without picking, pull the finger off to sound the second (lower) note.

LEGATO SLIDE: Strike the first note and then slide the same fret-hand finger up or down to the second note. The second note is not struck.

SHIFT SLIDE: Same as legato slide, except the second note is struck.

TRILL: Very rapidly alternate between the notes indicated by continuously hammering on and pulling off.

TREMOLO PICKING: The note is picked as rapidly and continuously as possible.

VIBRATO: The string is vibrated by rapidly bending and releasing the note with the fretting hand.

SHAKE: Using one finger, rapidly alternate between two notes on one string by sliding either a half-step above or below.

NATURAL HARMONIC: Strike the note while the fret hand lightly touches the string directly over the fret indicated.

MUFFLED STRINGS: A percussive sound is produced by laying the fret hand across the string(s) without depressing them and striking them with the pick hand.

BEND: Strike the note and bend up the interval shown.

BEND AND RELEASE: Strike the note and bend up as indicated, then release back to the original note. Only the first note is struck.

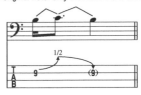

RIGHT-HAND TAP: Hammer ("tap") the fret indicated with the "pick-hand" index or middle finger and pull off to the note fretted by the fret hand.

LEFT-HAND TAP: Hammer ("tap") the fret indicated with the "fret-hand" index or middle finger.

SLAP: Strike ("slap") string with right-hand thumb.

POP: Snap ("pop") string with right-hand index or middle finger.

Additional Musical Definitions

	(accent)	• Accentuate note (play it louder).
	(accent)	• Accentuate note with great intensity.
	(staccato)	• Play the note short.
⊓		• Downstroke
V		• Upstroke

D.S. al Coda • Go back to the sign (%), then play until the measure marked "*To Coda*," then skip to the section labelled "**Coda**."

D.C. al Fine • Go back to the beginning of the song and play until the measure marked "*Fine*" (end).

Bass Fig. • Label used to recall a recurring pattern.

Fill • Label used to identify a brief melodic figure which is to be inserted into the arrangement.

tacet • Instrument is silent (drops out).

• Repeat measures between signs.

1. | 2. • When a repeated section has different endings, play the first ending only the first time and the second ending only the second time.

NOTE: Tablature numbers in parentheses mean:
1. The note is being sustained over a system (note in standard notation is tied), or
2. The note is sustained, but a new articulation (such as a hammer-on, pull-off, slide or vibrato) begins, or
3. The note is a barely audible "ghost" note (note in standard notation is also in parentheses).

All the Small Things

Words and Music by Tom De Longe and Mark Hoppus

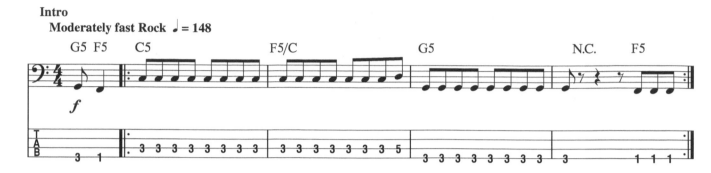

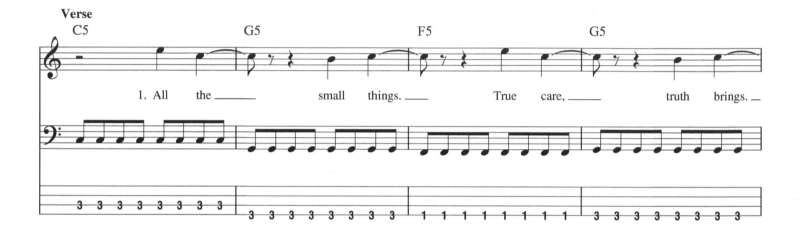

Watch - ing, _____ wait - ing, _____ com - mis - er - at - ing.

𝄋 Pre-Chorus

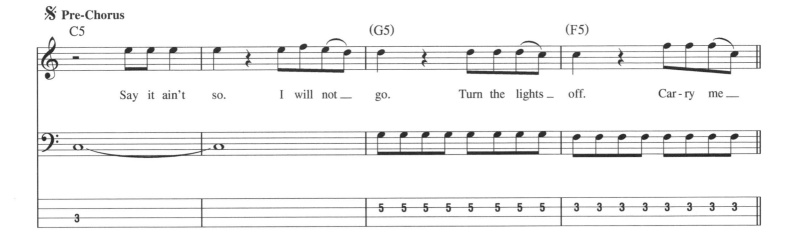

Say it ain't so. I will not _ go. Turn the lights _ off. Car - ry me _

Chorus

home.
Na, na, na, na, na, na, _____ na, na, na, na. Na na na na na na na, na, na, na.

To Coda 🜚

Na, na, na, na, na, na, _____ na, na, na, na. Na, na, na, na, na, na, _____ na, na, na, na.

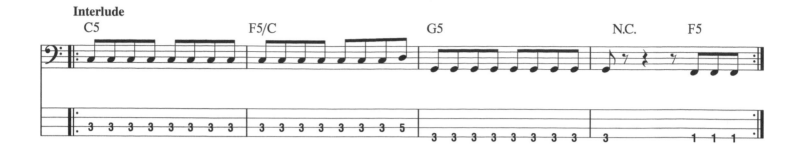

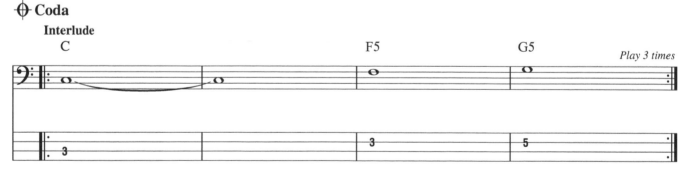

Outro

A Hard Day's Night

Words and Music by John Lennon and Paul McCartney

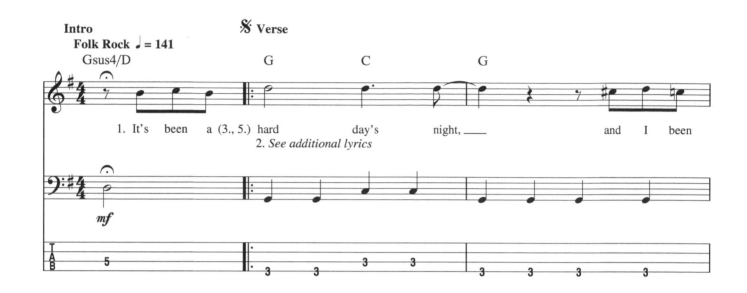

Chorus

1., 3., 4. get home to you ___ I find the things that you do ___ will make me feel ___ al - right. ___
2. *See additional lyrics*

1.

2. You know I ___ When I'm home ___ ev -'ry -thing seems ___ to be ___

Bridge

right. ___ When I'm home, ___

D.S. al Coda 1

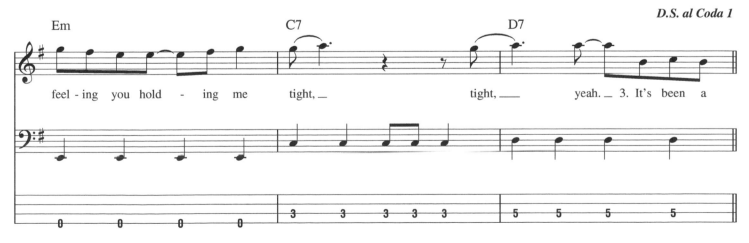

feel - ing you hold - ing me tight, ___ tight, ___ yeah. ___ 3. It's been a

⊕ Coda 1

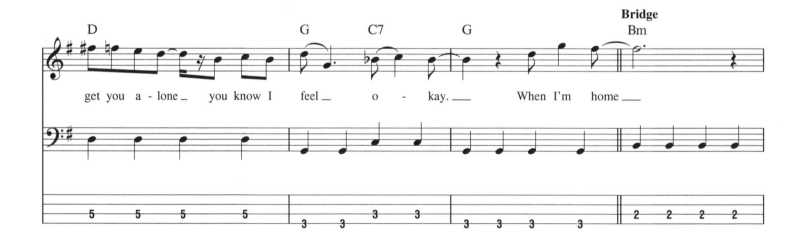

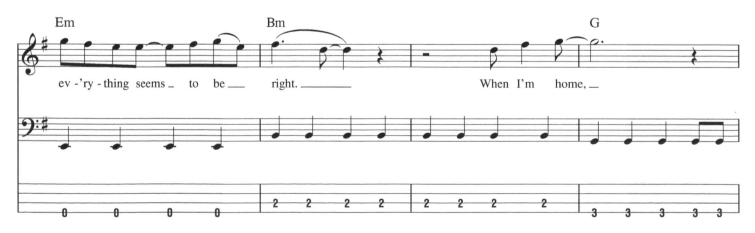

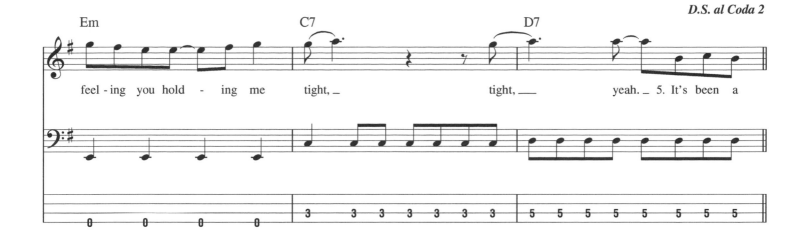

feel - ing you hold - ing me tight, ___ tight, ___ yeah. ___ 5. It's been a

⊕ Coda 2

Outro

You know I feel ___ al - right. ___ You know I

Fade out

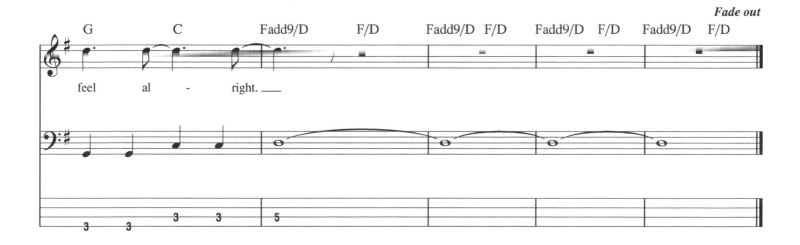

feel al - right. ___

Additional Lyrics

2. You know I work all day,
   To get you money to buy your things.
   And it's worth it just to hear you say
   You're gonna give me ev'rything.

Chorus 2. So why on earth should I moan
   'Cause when I get you alone
   You know I feel okay.

Roxanne

Music and Lyrics by Sting

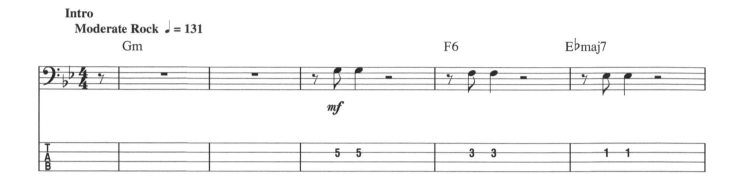

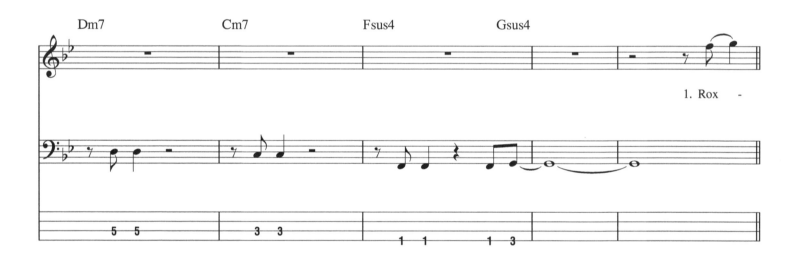

1. Rox -

anne,
2. *See additional lyrics*

you __ don't have to __ put on the __ red __ light. __

Those days are o - ver, you don't have to ____ sell your bod-y to the night. __ Rox -

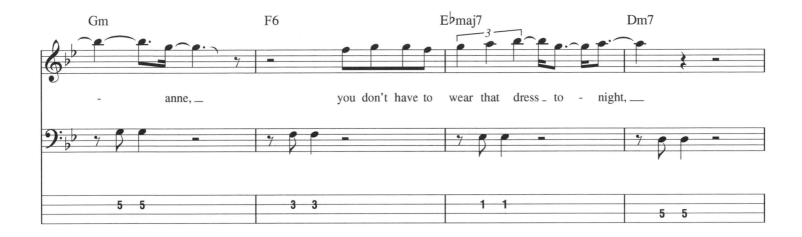

- anne, __ you don't have to wear that dress _ to - night, __

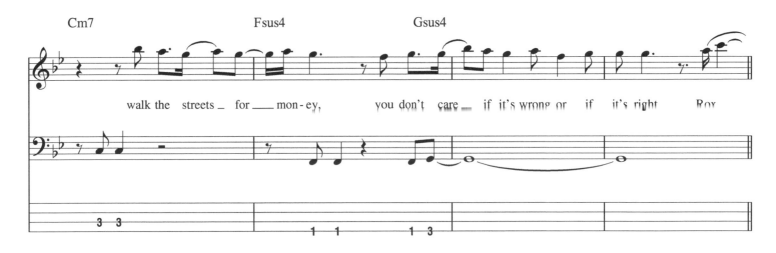

walk the streets _ for __ mon-ey, you don't care _ if it's wrong or if it's right Rox -

Pre-Chorus

- anne, ___ you don't have to put on the red ____ light. ___ Rox -

Additional Lyrics

2. I loved you since I knew ya.
   I wouldn't talk down to ya.
   I have to tell you just how I feel.
   I won't share you with another boy.
   I know my mind is made up.
   So put away your makeup.
   Told you once, I won't tell you again.
   It's a bad way.

Runnin' with the Devil

Words and Music by David Lee Roth, Edward Van Halen, Alex Van Halen and Michael Anthony

Tune down 1/2 step:
(low to high) Eb-Ab-Db-Gb

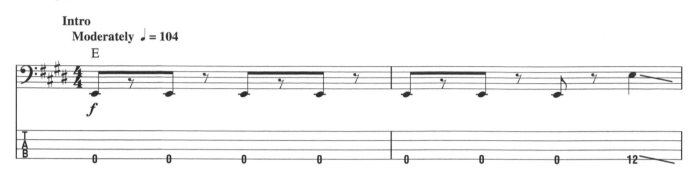

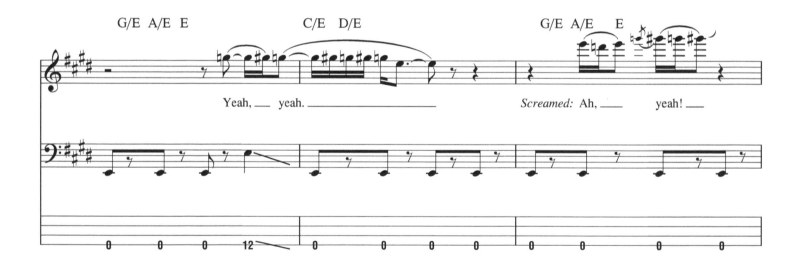

Yeah, — yeah. _____

Screamed: Ah, — yeah! —

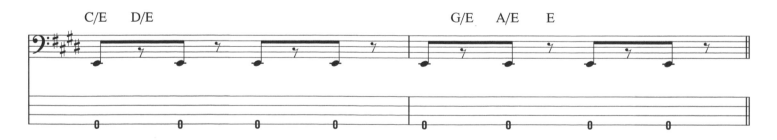

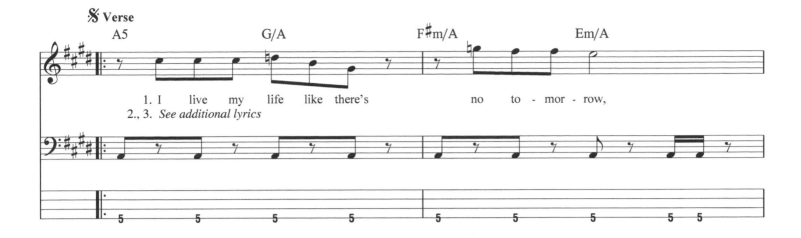

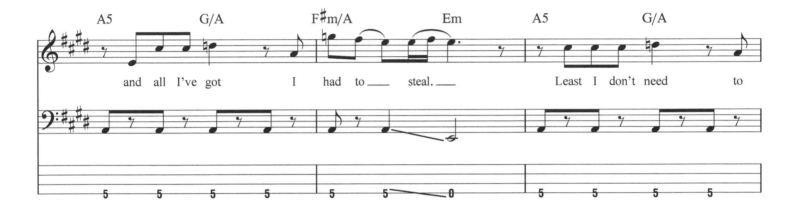

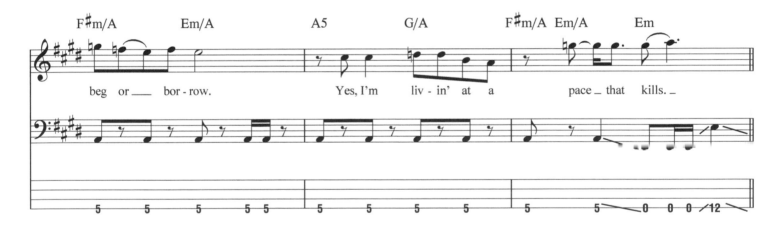

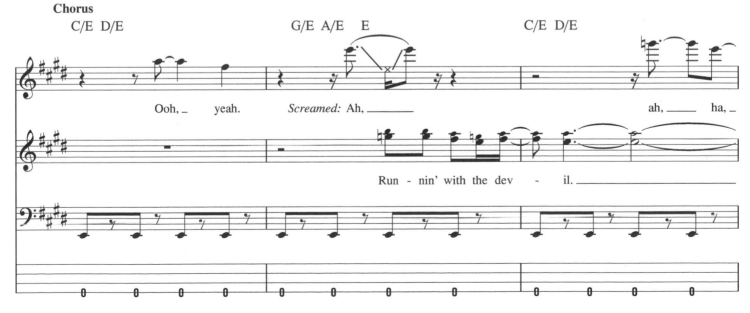

Additional Lyrics

2. I found the simple life ain't so simple
   When I jumped out on that road.
   I got no love, no love you'd call real.
   Ain't got nobody waitin' at home.

3. You know, I, I found the simple life weren't so simple, no,
   When I jumped out on that road.
   Got no love, no love you'd call real.
   Got nobody waitin' at home.

Smells Like Teen Spirit

Words and Music by Kurt Cobain, Krist Novoselic and Dave Grohl

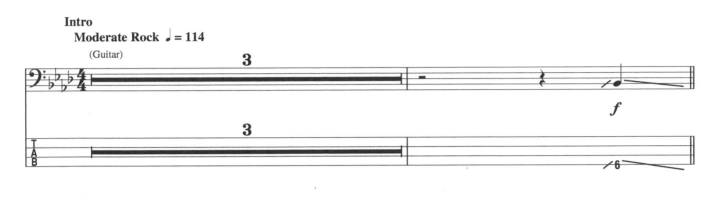

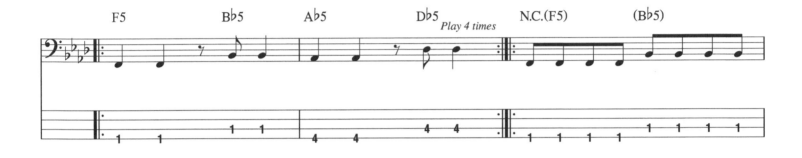

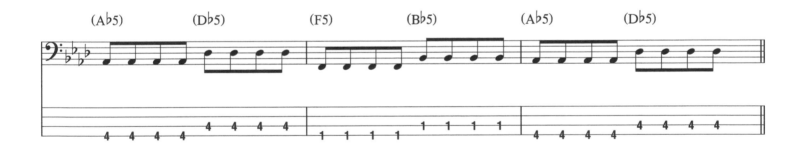

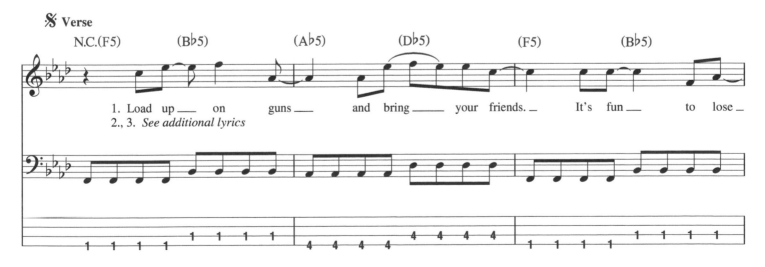

1. Load up __ on guns __ and bring __ your friends. __ It's fun __ to lose __
2., 3. *See additional lyrics*

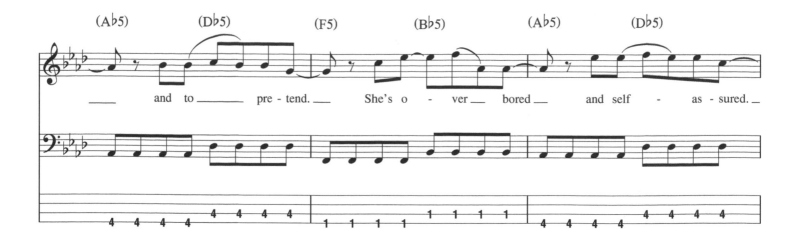

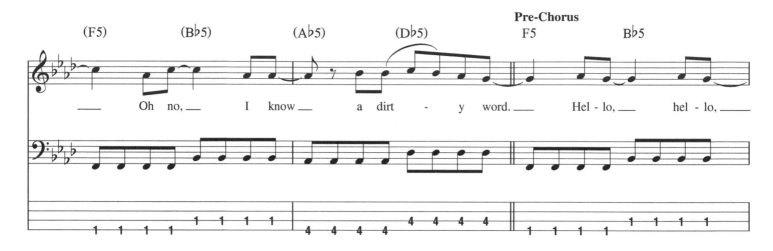

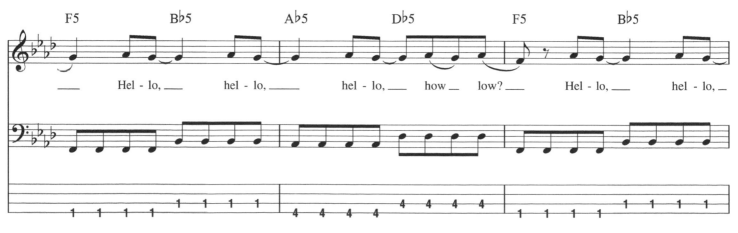

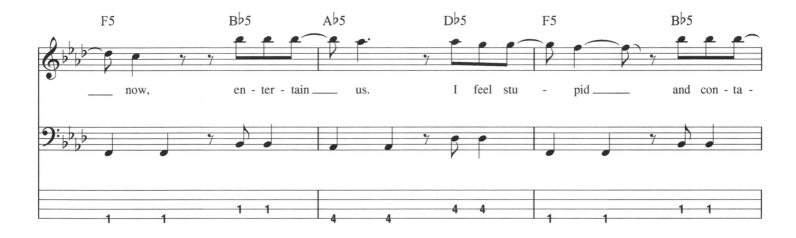

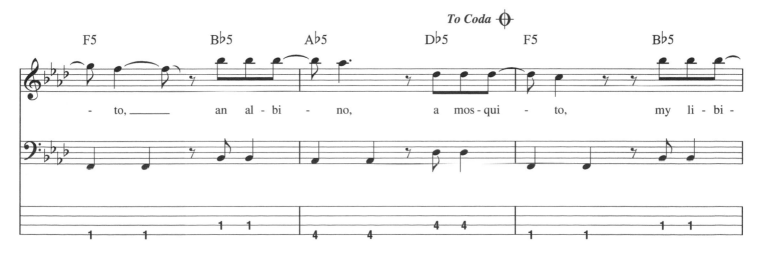

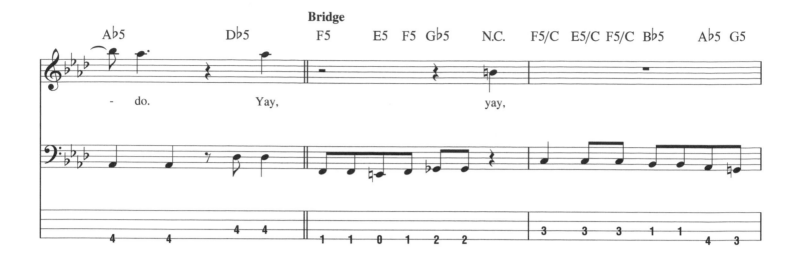

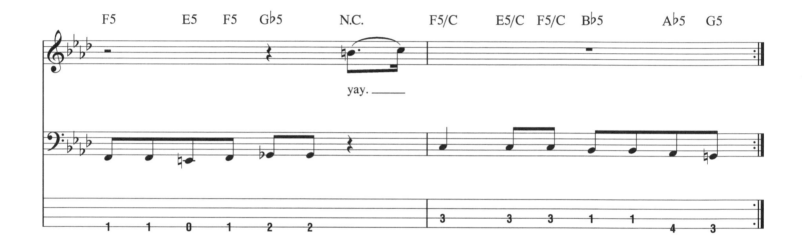

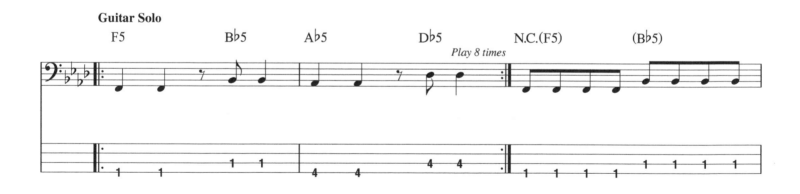

⊕ Coda

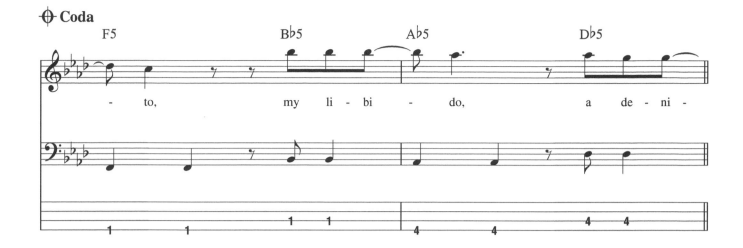

- to, my li - bi - do, a de - ni -

Outro

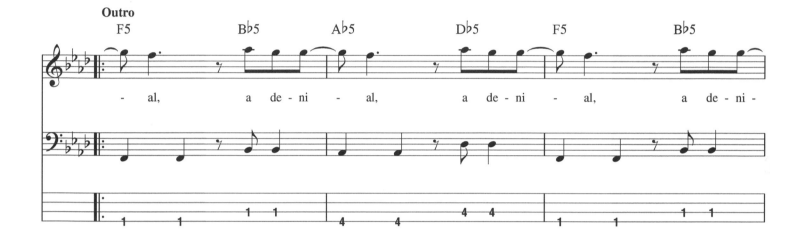

- al, a de - ni - al, a de - ni - al, a de - ni -

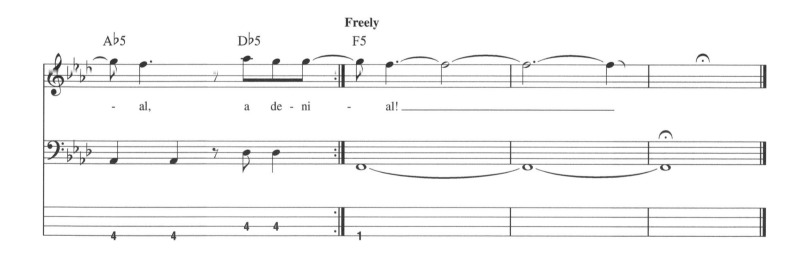

Freely

- al, a de - ni - al!

2. I'm worse at what I do best,
And for this gift I feel blessed.
Our little group has always been
And always will until the end.

3. And I forget just why I taste.
Oo, yeah, I guess it makes you smile,
I found it hard, it's hard to find.
Oh well, whatever, never mind.

Sunshine of Your Love

Words and Music by Jack Bruce, Pete Brown and Eric Clapton

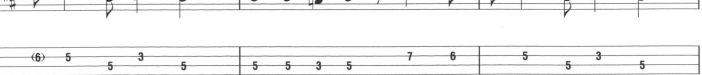

soon be with you __ my __ love, _____ to give you my dawn __ sur - prise. __

_____ I'll be with you dar - ling soon. _____ I'll

be with you when the stars start fall - ing

To Coda ⊕

Guitar Solo

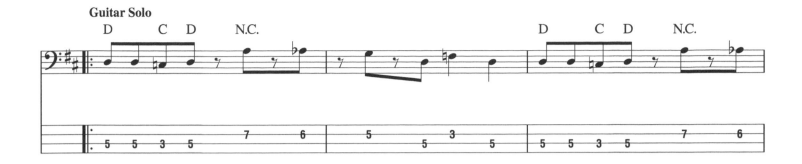

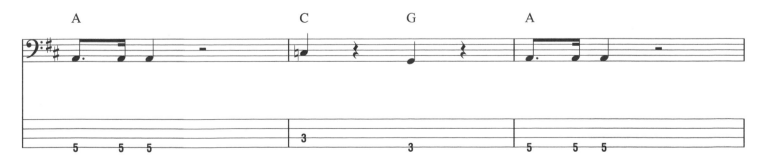

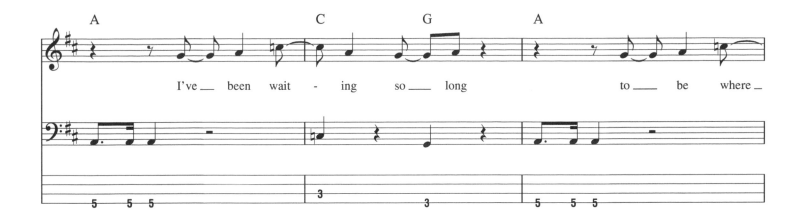

I've been wait-ing so long to be where

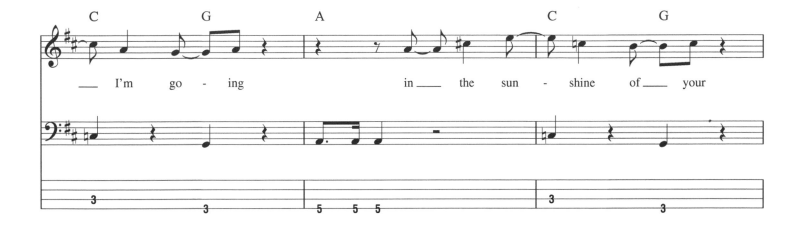

I'm go-ing in the sun-shine of your

Outro

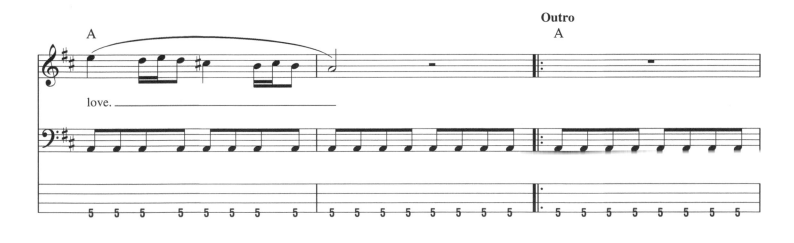

love.

Repeat and fade

Additional Lyrics

2., 3. I'm with you, my love;
The light shining through on you.
Yes, I'm with you, my love.
It's the morning and just we two.
I'll stay with you, darling, now.
I'll stay with you till my seeds are dried up.

Wild Thing

Words and Music by Chip Taylor

Intro
Moderate Rock ♩ = 102

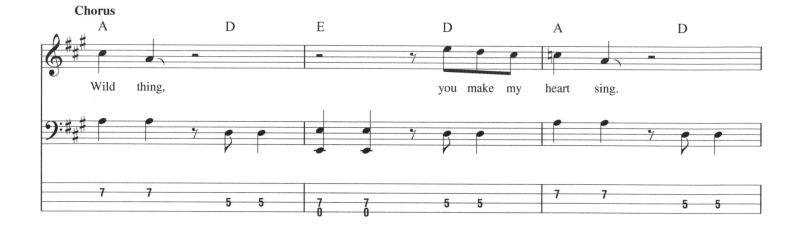

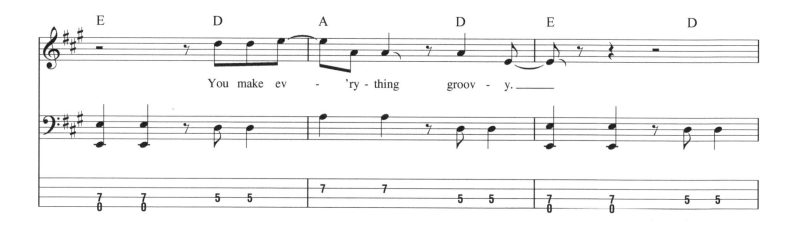

think I love you,
think you move me,
but I wan-na know ___ for sure.

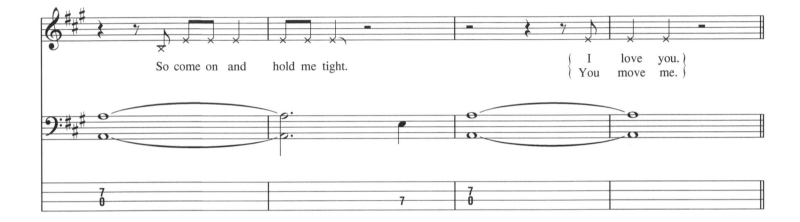

So come on and   hold me tight.

I   love   you.
You   move   me.

Pre-Chorus

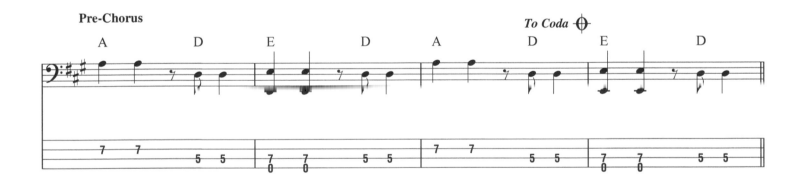

A   D   E   D   A   D   E   D

To Coda ⊕

Chorus

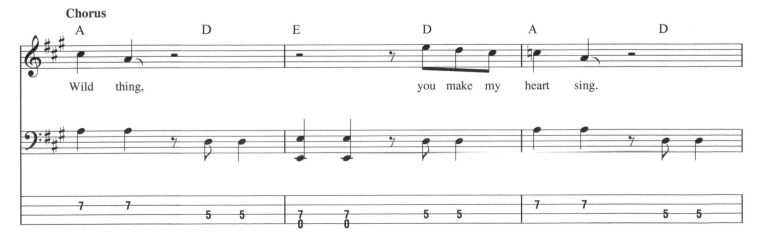

A   D   E   D   A   D

Wild   thing,   you make my   heart   sing.

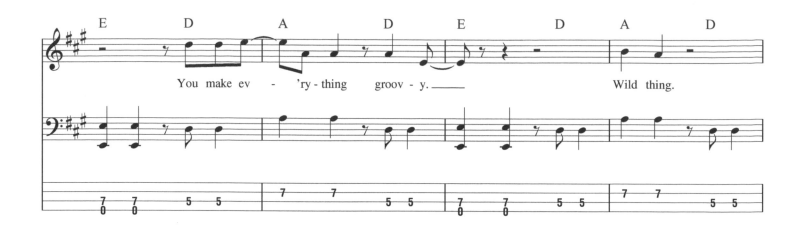

You make ev - - 'ry - thing groov - y. ___ Wild thing.

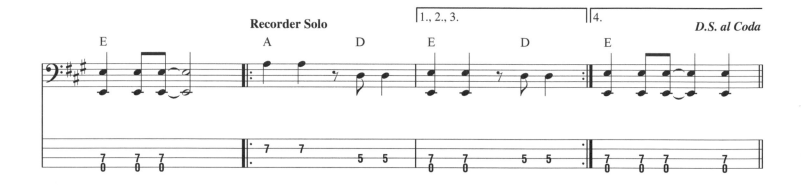

Recorder Solo

1., 2., 3.

4.

D.S. al Coda

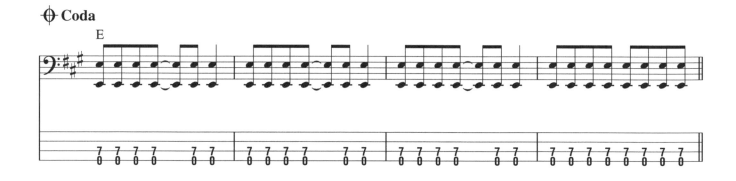

Coda

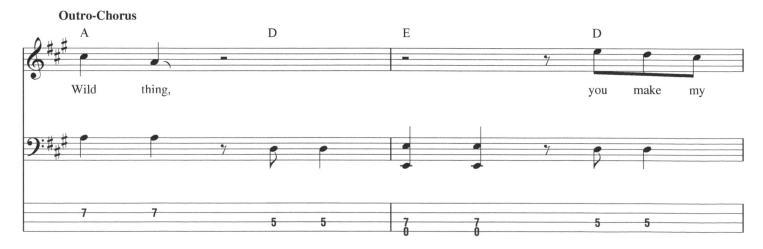

Outro-Chorus

Wild thing, you make my

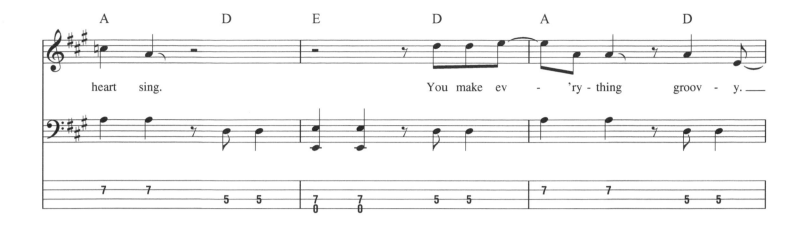

heart sing. You make ev - 'ry - thing groov - y. ___

___ Wild thing. Come on, ___ come on

Begin fade

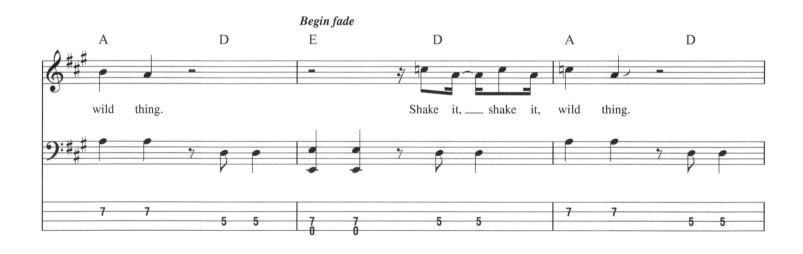

wild thing. Shake it, ___ shake it, wild thing.

Fade out

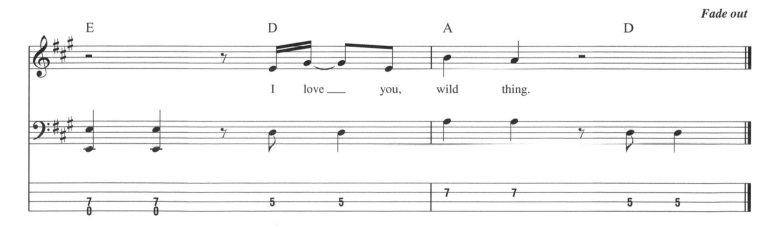

I love ___ you, wild thing.

37

With or Without You

Words by Bono and The Edge
Music by U2

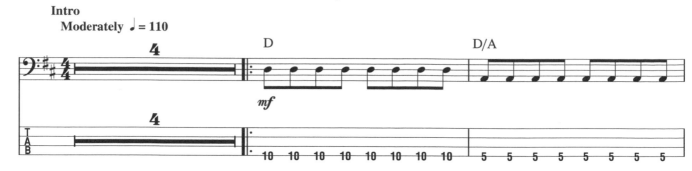

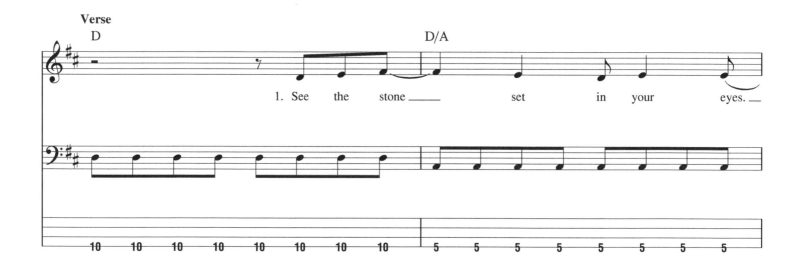

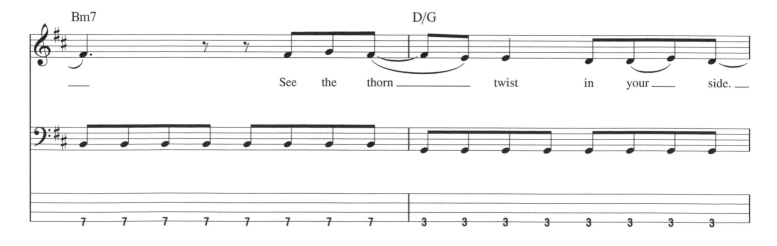

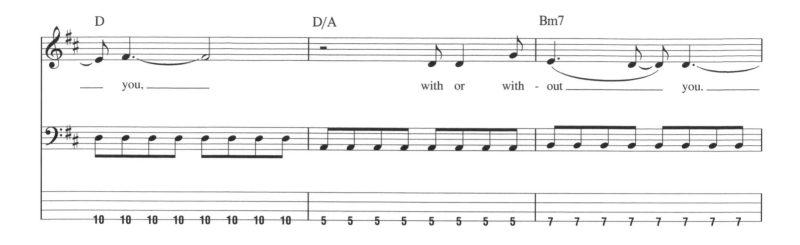

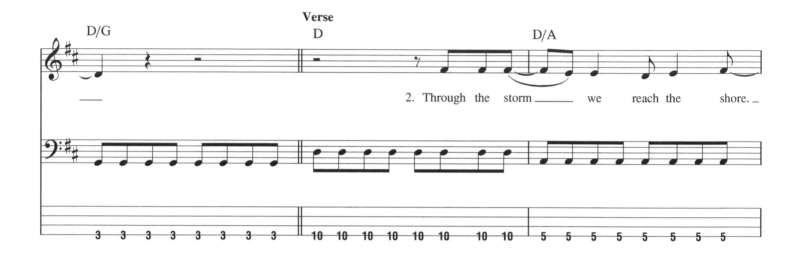

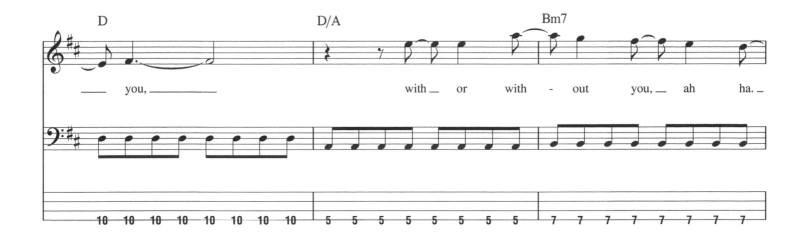

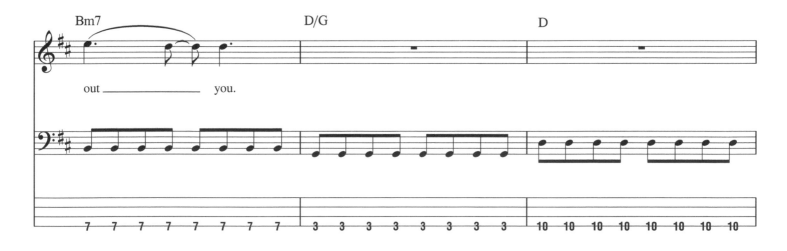

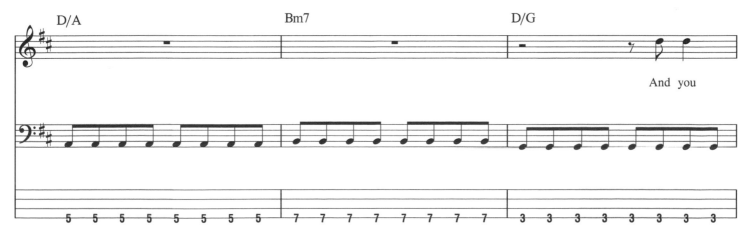

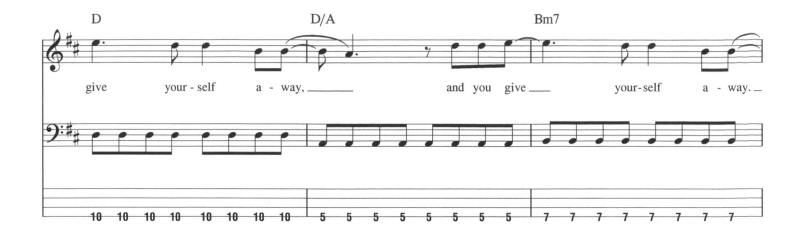

give your-self a - way, _____ and you give _____ your-self a - way. _____

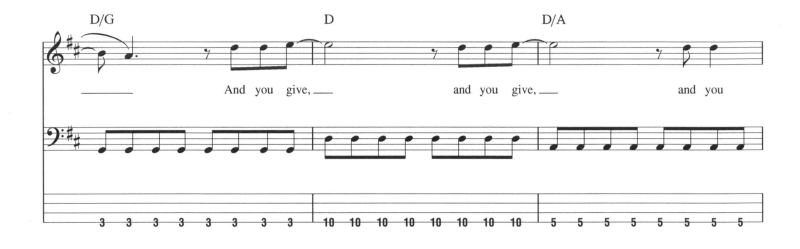

_____ And you give, _____ and you give, _____ and you

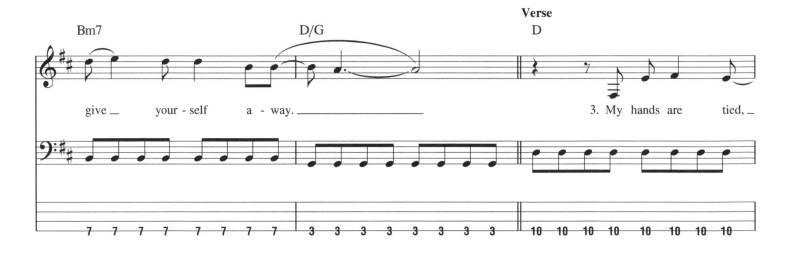

give _____ your-self a - way. _____ 3. My hands are tied, _____

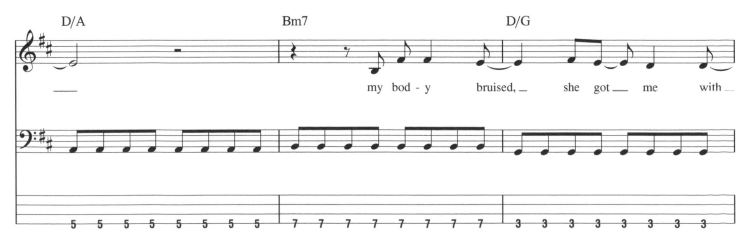

my bod - y bruised, _____ she got _____ me with _____

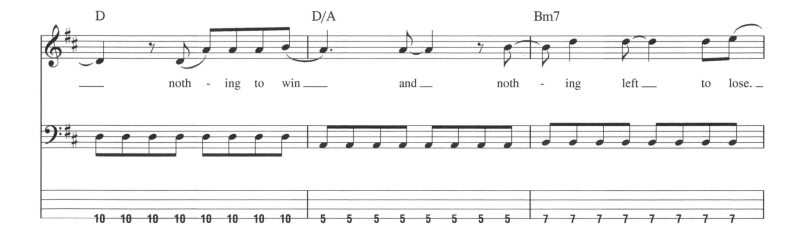

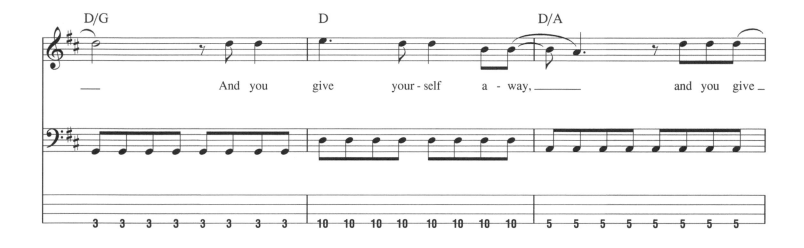

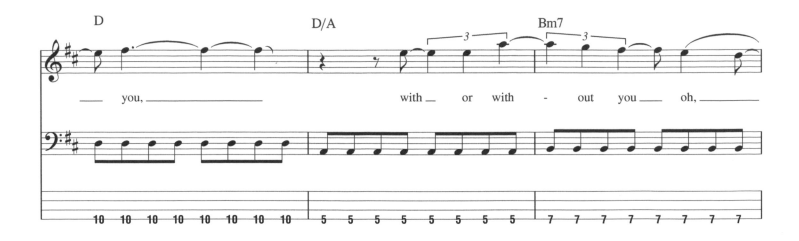

you, with or with - out you oh,

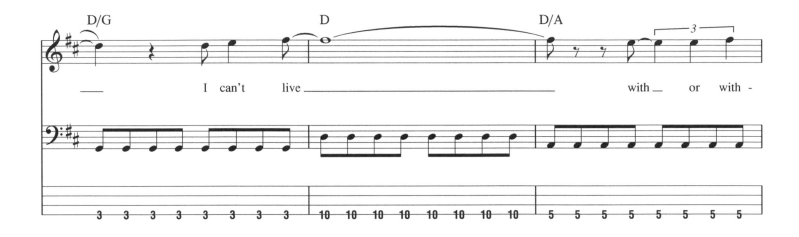

I can't live with or with -

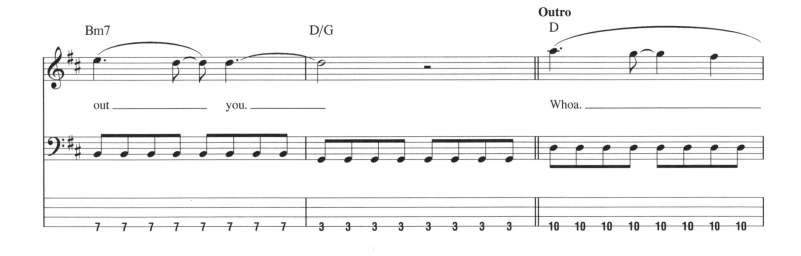

Outro

out you. Whoa.

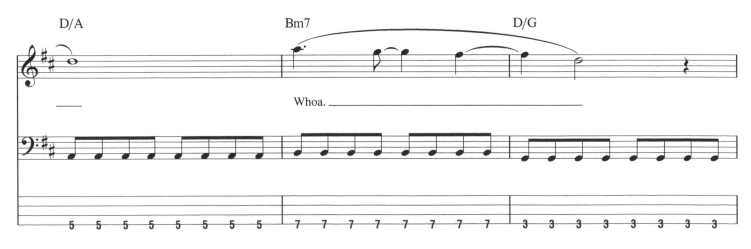

Whoa.

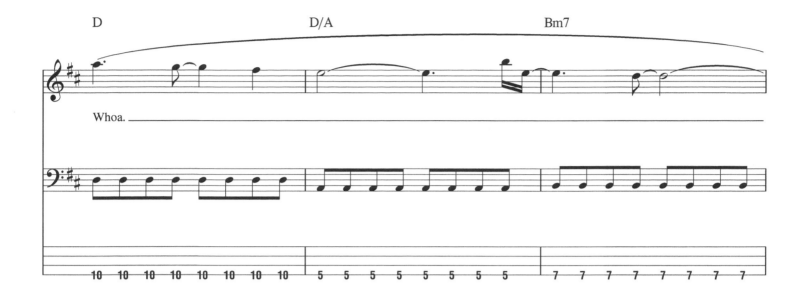

Whoa. _____

With or with-out _____ you, _____ with _____ or with -

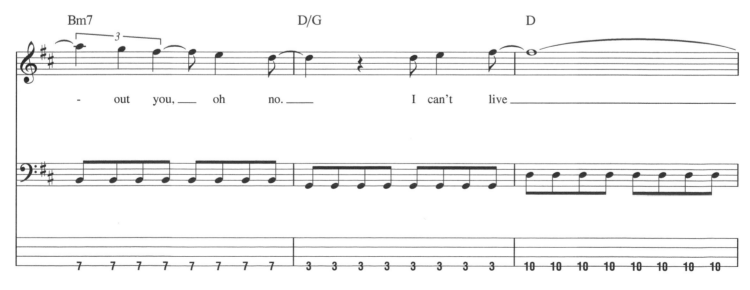

- out you, ____ oh no. ____ I can't live _____

with __ or with - out _____ you, _____ with or with -

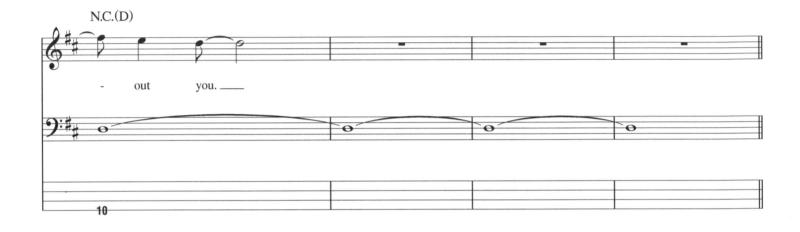

- out you. ____

Ooh. _____

Repeat and fade

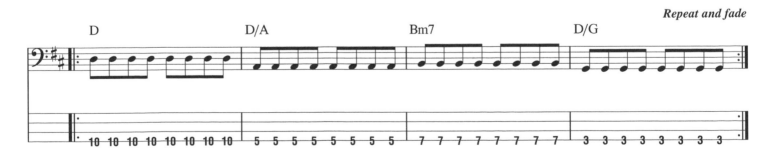

Hal•Leonard® BASS PLAY-ALONG

The Bass Play-Along™ Series will help you play your favorite songs quickly and easily! Just follow the tab, listen to the audio to hear how the bass should sound, and then play-along using the separate backing tracks. The melody and lyrics are also included in the book in case you want to sing, or to simply help you follow along. The audio files are enhanced so you can adjust the recording to any tempo without changing pitch!

Hal•Leonard®

Visit Hal Leonard Online at **www.halleonard.com**

BASS RECORDED VERSIONS

Bass Recorded Versions feature authentic transcriptions written in standard notation and tablature for bass guitar. This series features complete bass lines from the classics to contemporary superstars.

25 Essential Rock Bass Classics
00690210 / $19.99

Avenged Sevenfold – Nightmare
00691054 / $19.99

The Beatles – Abbey Road
00128336 / $24.99

The Beatles – 1962-1966
00690556 / $19.99

The Beatles – 1967-1970
00690557 / $24.99

Best of Bass Tab
00141806 / $17.99

The Best of Blink 182
00690549 / $18.99

Blues Bass Classics
00690291 / $22.99

Boston – Bass Collection
00690935 / $19.95

Stanley Clarke – Collection
00672307 / $22.99

Dream Theater – Bass Anthology
00119345 / $29.99

Funk Bass Bible
00690744 / $24.99

Hard Rock Bass Bible
00690746 / $22.99

**Jimi Hendrix –
Are You Experienced?**
00690371 / $17.95

Jimi Hendrix – Bass Tab Collection
00160505 / $24.99

Iron Maiden – Bass Anthology
00690867 / $24.99

Jazz Bass Classics
00102070 / $19.99

The Best of Kiss
00690080 / $22.99

**Lynyrd Skynyrd –
All-Time Greatest Hits**
00690956 / $24.99

Bob Marley – Bass Collection
00690568 / $24.99

Mastodon – Crack the Skye
00691007 / $19.99

Megadeth – Bass Anthology
00691191 / $22.99

Metal Bass Tabs
00103358 / $22.99

Best of Marcus Miller
00690811 / $24.99

Motown Bass Classics
00690253 / $19.99

Muse – Bass Tab Collection
00123275 / $22.99

Nirvana – Bass Collection
00690066 / $19.99

**Nothing More –
Guitar & Bass Collection**
00265439 / $24.99

The Offspring – Greatest Hits
00690809 / $17.95

The Essential Jaco Pastorius
00690420 / $22.99

**Jaco Pastorius –
Greatest Jazz Fusion Bass Player**
00690421 / $24.99

Pearl Jam – Ten
00694882 / $19.99

Pink Floyd – Dark Side of the Moon
00660172 / $17.99

The Best of Police
00660207 / $24.99

Pop/Rock Bass Bible
00690747 / $24.99

Queen – The Bass Collection
00690065 / $22.99

R&B Bass Bible
00690745 / $24.99

Rage Against the Machine
00690248 / $19.99

**Red Hot Chili Peppers –
BloodSugarSexMagik**
00690064 / $19.99

**Red Hot Chili Peppers –
By the Way**
00690585 / $24.99

**Red Hot Chili Peppers –
Californication**
00690390 / $22.99

**Red Hot Chili Peppers –
Greatest Hits**
00690675 / $22.99

**Red Hot Chili Peppers –
I'm with You**
00691167 / $22.99

**Red Hot Chili Peppers –
One Hot Minute**
00690091 / $22.99

**Red Hot Chili Peppers –
Stadium Arcadium**
00690853 / Book Only $24.95

Rock Bass Bible
00690446 / $22.99

Rolling Stones – Bass Collection
00690256 / $24.99

Royal Blood
00151826 / $24.99

**Rush – The Spirit of Radio:
Greatest Hits 1974-1987**
00323856 / $24.99

Best of Billy Sheehan
00173972 / $24.99

Slap Bass Bible
00159716 / $29.99

Sly & The Family Stone for Bass
00109733 / $22.99

Best of Yes
00103044 / $24.99

Best of ZZ Top for Bass
00691069 / $24.99

HAL•LEONARD®

Visit Hal Leonard Online at
www.halleonard.com

Prices, contents & availability subject to change without notice.
Some products may not be available outside the U.S.A.